First World War
and Army of Occupation
War Diary
France, Belgium and Germany

42 DIVISION
Headquarters, Branches and Services
Royal Army Veterinary Corps
Deputy Assistant Director Veterinary Services
2 March 1917 - 31 March 1919

WO95/2648/4

The Naval & Military Press Ltd
www.nmarchive.com
Published in association with The National Archives

Published by

The Naval & Military Press Ltd

Unit 10 Ridgewood Industrial Park,

Uckfield, East Sussex,

TN22 5QE England

Tel: +44 (0) 1825 749494

www.naval-military-press.com

www.nmarchive.com

This diary has been reprinted in facsimile from the original. Any imperfections are inevitably reproduced and the quality may fall short of modern type and cartographic standards.

© **Crown Copyright**
Images reproduced by permission of The National Archives, London, England, 2015.

Contents

Document type	Place/Title	Date From	Date To
Heading	WO95/2648/4		
Heading	42nd Division D.A. Dir. Vety Services Mar 1917-Mar 1919		
Heading	42nd (East Lancs) Division War Diary Volume (1) March 1st To March 31st 1917		
War Diary	Marseilles	02/03/1917	04/03/1917
War Diary	Pont Remy	06/03/1917	06/03/1917
War Diary	Hallencourt	07/03/1917	27/03/1917
Heading	42nd (East Lancs) Division War Diary Volume (2) April 1st to April 30th 1917		
War Diary	Hallencourt	02/04/1917	02/04/1917
War Diary	Mericourt-Sur-Somme	04/04/1917	14/04/1917
War Diary	Peronne	23/04/1917	24/04/1917
Heading	42nd (East Lancs) Division War Diary Volume (2) May 1st to May 31st 1917		
War Diary	Peronne	01/05/1917	03/05/1917
War Diary	Roisel	04/05/1917	07/05/1917
War Diary	Brusle	19/05/1917	23/05/1917
War Diary	Ytres	25/05/1917	31/05/1917
Heading	42nd (East Lancs) Division War Diary Volume 4 June 1st to June 30th		
War Diary	Ytres 57 1/10,000 P 26th	04/06/1917	23/06/1917
Heading	42nd (East Lancs) Division War Diary Volume 5 July 1st 1917 to July 31st 1917		
War Diary	Ytres 57c P26 62.7	01/07/1917	09/07/1917
War Diary	Achiet-Le-Petit 57c G 14 C	14/07/1917	29/07/1917
Heading	War Diary Volume 6 Month August 1917 DADVS 42nd Division		
War Diary	Achiet Le Petit 57c C14c	04/08/1917	15/08/1917
War Diary	Acheux	21/08/1917	21/08/1917
War Diary	Albert	22/08/1917	23/08/1917
War Diary	Watou Sheet 27 1/40,000 K4B 3.6	25/08/1917	31/08/1917
Heading	War Diary Volume IX Sept 1st to Sept 30th 1917 D.A.D.V.S. 42nd Division		
War Diary	Sheet 28 1/40,000 H7 C 8.5	01/09/1917	17/09/1917
War Diary	Poperinghe Sheet 28 1/40000 GI.d 5.6	18/09/1917	21/09/1917
War Diary	La Panne Sheet 11 W. 14 D. 5.5	23/09/1917	23/09/1917
War Diary	St Idesbalde Sheet II W. 10b 6.7	25/09/1917	29/09/1917
Heading	42nd (East Lancs) Division War Diary Volume (8) October 1st to October 31st 1917		
War Diary	St. Idesbalde Sheet II 1/40,000 Wid I 5.6	02/10/1917	02/10/1917
War Diary	Coxyde Bains Sheet XI 1/40000 W 6c O.3.3	07/10/1917	25/10/1917
Heading	42nd (East Lancs) Division War Diary Volume 9 Nov 1st to Nov 30th 1917		
War Diary	Coxyde Bains Sheet XI 1/40000 W6 C 3.3	01/11/1917	19/11/1917
War Diary	Aire Sheet 36 1/40000 H28 D.22	22/11/1917	29/11/1917
War Diary	Locon	30/11/1917	30/11/1917
Heading	42nd (East Lancs) Division War Diary Volume 9 Dec 1st to Dec 31st 1917		
War Diary	Locon	01/12/1917	01/12/1917

War Diary	Bathune Combined Sheet 36 SE 36 SW 36 NE 36 NW 1/40000 X 7c 8.8	06/12/1917	29/12/1917
Heading	War Diary D.A.D.V.S 42nd Division January 1st 1918 to January 31st 1918 Volume 1		
War Diary	Locon	05/01/1918	05/01/1918
War Diary	Bethune Combined Sheet	07/01/1918	07/01/1918
War Diary	36a SE 36 SW	08/01/1918	08/01/1918
War Diary	36 B N.E. 36 NW 1/40,000 X7c 8.8	12/01/1918	31/01/1918
War Diary	D.A.D.V.S. 42nd Division War Diary Volume 2 Feb 1st to Feb 28th 1918		
War Diary	Locon	02/02/1918	02/02/1918
War Diary	Bethune Combined Sheet 36a SE 36 NW 36 B NE 36 NW 1/40000 X7 C 8.8	09/02/1918	15/02/1918
War Diary	Hinges Wl6 10.65	19/02/1918	23/02/1918
Heading	D.A.D.V.S. 42nd Division War Diary Volume 3 March 1st to March 31st 1918		
War Diary	Hinges	01/03/1918	01/03/1918
War Diary	Bethune Combined Sheet 26a SE 36 SW 36 NE 36 C NW 1/40000 W16a 25	02/03/1918	05/03/1918
War Diary	La Beuvriere D11. D 2.2	06/03/1918	23/03/1918
War Diary	St Amand. Sheet 57d	23/03/1918	31/03/1918
Heading	D.A.D.V.S. 42nd Division War Diary Volume 4 April 1st to April 30th 1918		
War Diary	St Amand. Sheet 5 d d10 c 5.5	02/04/1918	02/04/1918
War Diary	Henu	04/04/1918	07/04/1918
War Diary	Pas	08/04/1918	16/04/1918
War Diary	Couin	17/04/1918	30/04/1918
Heading	D.A.D.V.S. 42nd Division War Diary Volume 5 May1st 1918 to May 31st 1918		
War Diary	Couin Sheet 57 D J1d 6.3	02/05/1918	06/05/1918
War Diary	Pas	09/05/1918	30/05/1918
Heading	D.A.D.V.S. 42nd Division War Diary Volume 6 June 1st 1918 to June 30th 1918		
War Diary	Pas Sheet 57D C16a 2.3	01/06/1918	06/06/1918
War Diary	Bus-Les Artois Sheet 57.9 J.26.a.9.3	07/06/1918	30/06/1918
Heading	War Diary Volume 7 From 1.7.18 To 31.7.18 D.A.D.V.S. 42nd Division		
War Diary	Bus-Les-Artois	03/07/1918	09/07/1918
War Diary	Sarton	11/07/1918	27/07/1918
Heading	War Diary Volume 8 August 1st to August 31st 1918 D.A.D.V.S 42nd Division		
War Diary	Authie Sheet 57D 1/40000 1.16a 3.2	01/09/1918	15/09/1918
War Diary	Bus	17/09/1918	30/09/1918
Heading	War Diary Volume 9 from 1.9.18 to 30.9.18 D.A.D.V.S. 42nd Division		
War Diary	Miraumont Sheet 57d L 35 C 5.3	02/09/1918	05/09/1918
War Diary	Pys	05/09/1918	21/09/1918
War Diary	Lebucquiere	24/09/1918	24/09/1918
Heading	War Diary Volume 10 from 1/10/18 to 31/10/18 D.A.D.V.S 42nd Division		
War Diary	Lebucquiere	01/10/1918	01/10/1918
War Diary	I 36.d.8.1	02/10/1918	09/10/1918
War Diary	Esnes	10/10/1918	12/10/1918
War Diary	Beauvois	13/10/1918	31/10/1918
Heading	War Diary Volume II from 1/11/18 to 30/11/18 D.A.D.V.S. 42nd Division		

War Diary	Beauvois	01/11/1918	05/11/1918
War Diary	Le Quesnoy	06/11/1918	10/11/1918
War Diary	Hautmont	11/11/1918	30/11/1918
Heading	War Diary Volume 12 D.A.D.V.S 42nd Division from 1/12/18 to 31/12/18		
War Diary	Hautmont	01/12/1918	15/12/1918
War Diary	Binche	16/12/1918	16/12/1918
War Diary	Fontaine l'Eveque	17/12/1918	18/12/1918
War Diary	Charleroi	19/12/1918	31/12/1918
Heading	War Diary D.A.D.V.S 42nd Division Volume 1 from Jan 1st 1919 Jan 31st 1919		
War Diary	Charleroi	01/01/1919	31/01/1919
Heading	War Diary D.A.D.V.S 42nd Division Volume 2 from 1/2/19 to 28/2/19		
War Diary	Charleroi	01/02/1919	28/02/1919
Heading	War Diary Volume 3 D.A.D.V.S 42nd Division 1/3/19 to 31/3/19		
War Diary	Charleroi	01/03/1919	31/03/1919

wo 95
2648/4

42ND DIVISION

D. A. DIR. VETY SERVICES
MAR 1917-MAR 1919

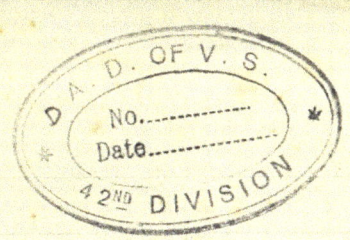

Confidential

42nd (East Lancs.) Division

War Diary

Volume (1)

March 1st to March 31st 1917.

Army Form C. 2118

WAR DIARY
OF
INTELLIGENCE SUMMARY
(Erase heading not required.)

A.D.V.S.
42nd Division.

Instructions regarding War Diaries and Intelligence Summaries are contained in F.S. Regs., Part II. and the Staff Manual respectively. Title Pages will be prepared in manuscript.

Place	Date	Hour	Summary of Events and Information	Remarks and references to Appendices
MARSEILLES	2-3-17		Disembarked H.M.T. "Transylvania" from Egypt. B	
	4-3-17		Entrained at Marseilles. B	
PONT REMY	6-3-17		Arrived at Pont Remy (Map France 1/100.000 Abbeville 14) B	
HALLENCOURT	7-3-17		Joined D.H.Q. at Hallencourt (Map France 1/100.000 Dieppe 16) B	
	9-3-17		D.V.S. Fourth Army arrived at Office B	
	10-3-17		D.V.S. who is arranged moving in France to be based with Stallions B	
	14-3-17		Attended conference of A.D.V.S. at Fourth Army Headquarters B	
	24-3-17		Above was time adopted. B	
	25-3-17		Rec'd of application from DDVS with reference to assist by French to agents in possession of instructional orders for Stud of Stallions B	

J. Gillies Major
A.D.V.S.
42nd Division.

Wt. W593/826 1,000,000 4/15 J.B.C. & A. A.D.S.S./Forms/C. 2118.

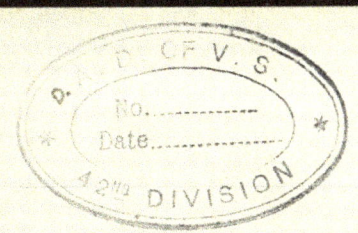

Confidential

42ND (East Lancs.) DIVISION

WAR DIARY

VOLUME (2)

APRIL 1st to APRIL 30th 1917.

WAR DIARY
or
INTELLIGENCE SUMMARY

(Erase heading not required.)

Army Form C. 2118

A.D.V.S. 42nd Division.

Instructions regarding War Diaries and Intelligence Summaries are contained in F. S. Regs., Part II. and the Staff Manual respectively. Title Pages will be prepared in manuscript.

Place	Date	Hour	Summary of Events and Information	Remarks and references to Appendices
HALLECOURT	2-4-17		Moved to Mericourt-sur-Somme (Map France 40,000 Sheet 62ᵈ b 6c.) J.	
MERICOURT	6-4-17		36 Horses hated with Mallein. Result negative. J.	
SUR-SOMME	14-4-17		Moved to Peronne. (Map France 1/40,000 Sheet 62ᵈ I 27b.) J.	
PERONNE	23-4-17		Endorsed for 10 days leave. J.	
	27-4-17		2 Horses lightly injured by bomb from hostile aircraft. 211ᵗʰ Brigade R.F.A. at Templeux-la-Fosse (Map France 1/40,000 Sheet 62ᶜ D 28d.) J.	

Jos. Gillies Major
A.D.V.S. 42nd Division.

42ND (East Lancs.) DIVISION.

WAR DIARY.

VOLUME (3)

MAY 1ST to MAY 31ST 1917

WAR DIARY
or
INTELLIGENCE SUMMARY

(Erase heading not required.)

Army Form C. 2118

A.D.V.S.
42ND DIVISION

Instructions regarding War Diaries and Intelligence Summaries are contained in F.S. Regs., Part II. and the Staff Manual respectively. Title Pages will be prepared in manuscript.

Place	Date	Hour	Summary of Events and Information	Remarks and references to Appendices
PERONNE	1.5.17		5th Army received a bad G.L. by letter 216. Brigade R.S.A. (Map France 1/40,000 Sheet 62D 1.2)	
	3.5.17		A.D.V.S. attended conference at Fourth Army Headquarters.	
ROISEL	4.5.17		Moved to ROISEL. (Map France 1/40,000 Sheet 62D K.11) ordered to carry out veterinary inspection D.A.C. 187 Horses tested with MALLEIN. Result Negative (Map France 1/10,000 Sheet 62D F.1a)	
			236th Infantry Brigade of Enemy (Map France 1/40,000 Sheet 62D F.1a)	
	5.5.17		59 Horses tested with MALLEIN. Result Negative.	
	6.5.17		62 Horses tested with MALLEIN. Result Negative.	
	7.5.17		72 Horses tested with MALLEIN. Result Negative.	
BRUSLE	19.5.17		Moved to BRUSLE (Map France 1/40,000 Sheet 62D J.34.b)	
	28.5.17		Moved to LITTLE WOOD, YPRES. (Map France 1/40,000 Sheet 57D C.26.d)	
YPRES	19.5.17		242 Horses tested with MALLEIN. Result Negative.	
	20.5.17		293 Horses tested with MALLEIN. Result Negative.	
	22.5.17		178 Horses tested with MALLEIN. Result Negative.	
	27.5.17		173 Horses tested with MALLEIN. Result Negative.	
	28.5.17		237 Horses tested with MALLEIN. Result Negative.	
	29.5.17		136 Horses tested with MALLEIN. Result Negative.	
	30.5.17		67 Horses tested with MALLEIN. Result Negative.	
	30.5.17		Lecture & Demonstration to the A.V.C. Personnel on the use of Anti-Gas Horse Respirators.	

Jos. Gillies, Major.
A.D.V.S., 42nd Division.

Confidential

D.A.D.V.S. 42ND (EAST LANCS) DIVISION

WAR DIARY

VOLUME 4

JUNE 1ST to JUNE 30TH.

WAR DIARY
or
INTELLIGENCE SUMMARY

(Erase heading not required.)

Army Form C. 2118

D.A.D.V.S.
42ⁿᵈ Division.

Instructions regarding War Diaries and Intelligence Summaries are contained in F. S. Regs., Part II. and the Staff Manual respectively. Title Pages will be prepared in manuscript.

Place	Date	Hour	Summary of Events and Information	Remarks and references to Appendices
YPRES 57ᵈ/10.c.10 P26.	4-6-17		Circular from D.D.V.S. FOURTH ARMY giving instructions for use of ANTI-GAS HORSE RESPIRATOR. CERTIFICATE forwarded that all V.Os and A.V.C. SERGEANTS instructed and have actually fixed on the Respirators.	
	4-6-17		Two HORSES wounded while grazing at 57d. O.28.a owing to a horse treading on and exploding an enemy bomb. The Horses were held in charge by the 3 Section of the D.A.C.	
	14-6-17		Letter from D.A.Q.M.G. 42ⁿᵈ Division forwarding authority for reduction of Horses of 197ᵗʰ MOBILE VETERINARY SECTION from 24 to 19. (Authority B.M.G. C.H.Q. 63144(Q.A.1)3 dated 22-6-17).	
	23-6-17		Letter from D.D.V.S. FOURTH ARMY. Owing to the re-organization of the system of Veterinary Administration in France the title of A.D.V.S. DIVISIONS has been altered to D.A.D.V.S. (Authority W.O. 121/depots/300(S.D.2) dated 13-6-17).	

Jos: Gillies Major
D.A.D.V.S. 42ⁿᵈ DIVISION

D.A.D.V.S 42ND (EAST. LANCS) DIVISION

WAR DIARY

VOLUME 5

JULY 1ST 1917 to JULY 31ST 1917.

Army Form C. 2118.

WAR DIARY
or
INTELLIGENCE SUMMARY
(Erase heading not required.)

D.A.D.V.S.
42ⁿᵈ DIVISION.

Instructions regarding War Diaries and Intelligence Summaries are contained in F. S. Regs., Part II. and the Staff Manual respectively. Title Pages will be prepared in manuscript.

Place	Date	Hour	Summary of Events and Information	Remarks and references to Appendices
YTRES 57ᶜ P26 b27	1·7·17		Had interview with A.D.V.S. III Corps, re Condition of Animals of Division. JJ.	
	4·7·17		100 Horses and 59 Mules arrived as Remounts for R.A. JJ.	
	7·7·17		Amendment to W.E. increasing personnel of M.V.S. by addition of Pte. Ast. Staff Sergt. JJ.	
	8·7·17		Moved from YTRES to ACHIET-LE-PETIT. Map Reference / Photo 57ᶜ G.14 e JJ.	
ACHIET-LE-PETIT 57ᶜ G.14 c	14·7·17 15·7·17		Attended Conference held by A.D.V.S. VI Corps. JJ. Reorganisation of A.V.C. One V.O. to be withdrawn from Division. (D.D.V.S. III ARMY. V.6/12·7·17) JJ.	
	16·7·17		Arrival of 52 Remounts for Division. JJ. Had interview with A.D.V.S. VI Corps re R.A. Horses. JJ.	
	21·7·17		Capt. MacKie A.V.C. proceeded to 19th Veterinary Hospital. Rouen, in accordance with D.D.V.S. III Army V. 6d/12·7·17. JJ.	
	28·7·17		Attended Conference held by A.D.V.S. VI Corps. JJ.	
	29·7·17		Attended Conference held by A.D.V.S. VI Corps. JJ. A.D.V.S. VI Corps Inspected M.V.S. JJ.	

Jo. Gillies Major
D.A.D.V.S. 42ⁿᵈ DIVISION.

Confidential

War Diary

Volume 6

Month August 1917

DADVS 42nd Division

YA86

WAR DIARY or INTELLIGENCE SUMMARY

Army Form C. 2118

D.A.D.V.S.
42ND DIVISION.

(Erase heading not required.)

Instructions regarding War Diaries and Intelligence Summaries are contained in F. S. Regs., Part II. and the Staff Manual respectively. Title Pages will be prepared in manuscript.

Place	Date	Hour	Summary of Events and Information	Remarks and references to Appendices
ACHIET-LE-PETIT 39°C 14.c	6-8-17		Attended Conference held by A.D.V.S. VI Corps. G.	
	7-8-17		Attended with A.D.V.S. VI Corps when he selected mares other than H.O. suitable for breeding Army Remounts of the War G.	
	11-8-17		Attended Conference held by A.D.V.S. VI Corps. G.	
	14-8-17		Examined 35 Remounts. 26 Horses and 9 Mules. G.	
	15-8-17		Present at 50th Division M.V.S. when 5 Horses were treated for Mange by the Sulphur Vapour method. G.	
ACHEUX	21-8-17		Moved to ACHEUX. G.	
ALBERT	22-8-17		Moved to ALBERT. G.	
	23-8-17		Entrained at BEAUCOURT-sur-ANCRE. Detrained at PROVEN and billeted at WATOU. G.	
WATOU Sheet 27 Nord K.6.27 K.4.B.3.6	25-8-17		Had interview with A.D.V.S. XIV Corps re situation of M.V.S. and Veterinary Aid Posts. G.	
	28-8-17		2 Horses killed by Shell Fire. G.	
	29-8-17		1 Horses killed by Shell Fire. G.	
	31-8-17		Moved to H.Q. C.L.C.S. Sheet 28. 2 Mules killed by Shell Fire. G.	

Geo. Gillies Major.
D.A.D.V.S. 42nd Division

WAR DIARY

VOLUME ~~X~~ IX

Sept 1st to Sept 30th 1917.

D.A.D.V.S
42nd Division

WAR DIARY or INTELLIGENCE SUMMARY

Army Form C. 2118

D.A.D.V.S.
42ND DIVISION.

Place	Date	Hour	Summary of Events and Information	Remarks and references to Appendices
Abeele/Hand	1-4-17		2 Mules killed by Shellfire.	
H.Q. C.E.F.	2-4-17		2 Mules and 2 Horses wounded by Shellfire.	
	3-4-17		1 Horse killed and 2 wounded by Shellfire. Examined 36 Remounts (24 L.D. Horses. 11 H.D. Horses	
	4-4-17		2 Horses wounded by Bomb. and 1 Pack Mule)	
	5-4-17		1 Mule killed and 1 Mule wounded by Shellfire.	
	6-4-17		1 Horse wounded by Shellfire.	
	7-4-17		2 Horses wounded and 1 killed by Shellfire.	
	8-4-17		3 Horses and 3 mules wounded by Bombs.	
	9-4-17		1 Horse wounded by Shellfire. 1 Horse and 1 Mule wounded by Bomb.	
	10-4-17		2 Mules killed by Shellfire.	
	11-4-17		Examined 13 Remounts (2 H.D. Horses and 12 L.D. Mules). 3 Horses wounded by Shellfire.	
	12-4-17		3 Horses killed and 1 wounded and 3 Gassed (Mustard) by Shellfire.	
	13-4-17		1 Mule wounded.	
	14-4-17		Attended Conference held by A.D.V.S. II Corps.	
	15-4-17		1 Mule killed, 3 Mules and 3 Horses wounded by Bomb. 2 Mules wounded by Shellfire.	
	16-4-17		Examined 77 Remounts for R.A. (33 Horses and 44 Mules).	
	17-4-17		1 Horse killed and 1 wounded by Shellfire.	
H.Poperinghe	18-4-17		Moved to Poperinghe. Shells 28 horses G.1 M.S.6. Capt J.R.Conchie A.V.C. arrived for duty.	
Hotel de Ville	19-4-17		6 Horses Gassed (Mustard).	
2 I.A.S.C.	20-4-17		Examined 48 Remounts (30 Horses and 18 Mules).	
La Panne	21-4-17		Moved to La Panne Sheet 11 horses W.H.D.S.S.	
Hotel de Malo	22-4-17		Reported H.A.D.V.S. II Corps.	
W.H.C.S.S.	23-4-17			

Army Form C. 2118

D.A.D.V.S.
42nd DIVISION.
SHEET No 2.

WAR DIARY
or
INTELLIGENCE SUMMARY
(Erase heading not required.)

Instructions regarding War Diaries and Intelligence Summaries are contained in F. S. Regs., Part II. and the Staff Manual respectively. Title Pages will be prepared in manuscript.

Place	Date	Hour	Summary of Events and Information	Remarks and references to Appendices
ST/DESBALDE Sheet 11. W.10.6.6.7.	25.4.17		Moved to ST IDESBALDE Sheet 11. W.10.6.6.7.8	
	29.4.17		Attended Conference held by A.D.V.S. XV Corps B	

J. Gillicoddyn
D.A.D.V.S. 42nd Division

1875 Wt. W593/826 1,000,000 4/15 J.B.C. & A. A.D.S.S./Forms/C. 2118.

D.A.D.V.S.
42ⁿᵈ Division.
WAR DIARY
VOLUME (8)

October 1ˢᵗ to October 31ˢᵗ 1917

D.A.D.V.S.,
42nd DIVISION.
No. V1369
Date 4/11/17

WAR DIARY

INTELLIGENCE SUMMARY

(Erase heading not required.)

D.A.D.V.S.
42ND DIVISION.

Army Form C. 2118

Place	Date	Hour	Summary of Events and Information	Remarks and references to Appendices
ST. IDESBALDE SHEET 11 M20.57 W10.2.3.6.	2.10.17		42ND DIVISIONAL ARTILLERY rejoined Division from YPRES. The night before their departure from YPRES (29.9.17) the following casualties occurred :- 17 HORSES KILLED BY BOMB. 2 HORSES KILLED BY SHELL FIRE. 31 HORSES WOUNDED BY BOMB, TEN OF WHICH HAD TO BE destroyed and 3 HORSES WOUNDED BY SHELL FIRE.	
COXYDE BAINS SHEET 27/20000 W6.0.3.3.	7.10.17		MOVED TO COXYDE BAINS.	
	11.10.17		9 HORSES KILLED BY SHELL FIRE. 6 HORSES WOUNDED BY SHELL FIRE. TWO of which had to be DESTROYED. 46 REMOUNTS (36 HORSES and 10 MULES) arrived.	
	18.10.17		9 HORSES WOUNDED BY SHELL FIRE 3 of which had to be DESTROYED. 128 REMOUNTS (95 HORSES and 33 MULES) arrived.	
	23.10.17		2 HORSES KILLED BY SHELL FIRE. 8 HORSES WOUNDED BY SHELL FIRE 2 of which	
	25.10.17		had to be DESTROYED.	

Joffillies Major
D.A.D.V.S. 42nd Division

D.A.D.V.S 42nd Division

WAR DIARY

VOLUME 9

Nov 1st to Nov 30th 1917.

WAR DIARY
or
INTELLIGENCE SUMMARY

D.A.D.V.S.
42ND DIVISION.

Army Form C. 2118

Place	Date	Hour	Summary of Events and Information	Remarks and references to Appendices
COXYDE BAINS Sheet II/40D W6 c 3.3	1-11-17		7 Horses Killed and 6 Horses Wounded (one of which had to be Destroyed) by Shell fire.	
	3-11-17		Attended Conference held by A.D.V.S. XV Corps.	
	8-11-17		2 Horses Wounded (both of which had to be Destroyed) by Shell fire.	
	10-11-17		Attended Conference held by A.D.V.S. XV Corps.	
	15-11-17		9 Horses Killed and 7 Horses Wounded by Shell fire.	
	17-11-17		Attended Conference held by A.D.V.S. XV Corps.	
	19-11-17		Moved to Aire. Sheet 36A from H.28.d.9.9.	
AIRE SHEET 36A H.28.d.9.9.	22-11-17		4 Horses Wounded (2 of which had to be Destroyed) by Shell fire.	
	29-11-17		Moved to Locon Sheet (combined) Bethune 36A S.E. 36 S.W. 36 N.E. 36 N.W. H.10 x7.9	
LOCON	30-11-17		25 Remounts (Horses) arrived for the Division.	

Jas Gillies Major
D.A.D.V.S. 42nd Division

D.A.D.V.S.
42nd Division
No. V.14.5.3.
Date 1/12/17

D.A.D.V.S

42ᴺᴰ Division

WAR DIARY

VOLUME (9)

Dec 1st 1917 to Dec 31st 1917

WAR DIARY
or
INTELLIGENCE SUMMARY

(Erase heading not required.)

Army Form C. 2118

D.A.D.V.S. 42ⁿᵈ Division.

Instructions regarding War Diaries and Intelligence Summaries are contained in F. S. Regs., Part II. and the Staff Manual respectively. Title Pages will be prepared in manuscript.

Place	Date	Hour	Summary of Events and Information	Remarks and references to Appendices
LOCON (centre point) Bethune sheet 26 S.E. 36 S.W. 36 N.E. 36 N.W. X7086	1-12-17		Attended Conference held by A.D.V.S. II Corps.	
	6-12-17		3 Horses killed by shell and one killed by gun shot.	
	11-12-17		Evacuated 83 Remounts (78 Horses and 5 Mules).	
	13-12-17		4 Horses killed and 5 Wounded (2 of which had to be destroyed) by shellfire.	
	20-12-17		Division transferred from II Corps to First Corps.	
	22-12-17		Attended Conference held by A.D.V.S. 1ˢᵗ Corps.	
	27-12-17		Examined 104 Remounts (all horses).	
	29-12-17		Attended Conference held by A.D.V.S. 1ˢᵗ Corps.	

J Williams Major
DADVS 42ⁿᵈ Division

WAR DIARY

D.A.D.V.S. 42nd DIVISION.

JANUARY 1st 1918 – JANUARY 31st 1918.

VOLUME I.

Army Form C. 2118

WAR DIARY
or
INTELLIGENCE SUMMARY
(Erase heading not required.)

D.A.D.V.S.
42ᴺᴰ DIVISION

Place	Date	Hour	Summary of Events and Information	Remarks and references to Appendices
LOCON.	5-1-18		Attended Conference held by A.D.V.S. 1ˢᵗ Corps. G	
BETHUNE	7-1-18		84ᵗʰ Army Field Artillery Brigade attached to Division for Administration G	
Bonturl Zhest	8-1-18		Examined 100 Remounts (all Horses) G	
36 S.E. 36 S.W.	12-1-18		Attended Conference held by A.D.V.S. 1ˢᵗ Corps. G	
36ᴮ N.E. 36ᴮ N.W.	17-1-18		One Horse Wounded by Shell and had to be Destroyed. G	
1/40,000 X7066	19-1-18		Attended Conference held by A.D.V.S. 1ˢᵗ Corps. G	
			268ᵗʰ Machine Gun Company joined Division G	
	22-1-18		43 Horses of 268ᵗʰ M.G. Coy tested with Mallein. No Reactors. G	
	23-1-18		11 Horses of 268ᵗʰ M.G. Coy tested with Mallein. No Reactors. G	
	24-1-18		423ʳᵈ Field Coy R.E. attached to Division replacing 422ⁿᵈ Field Coy R.E. G	
	26-1-18		Attended Conference held by A.D.V.S. 1ˢᵗ Corps. G	
	31-1-18		One Horse Wounded by Bomb. G	

Jo Gillies Major
D.A.D.V.S. 42ᴺᴰ DIVISION.

D.A.D.V.S.
42ⁿᵈ Division.
WAR DIARY
Volume 2

Feb 1ˢᵗ to Feb 28ᵗʰ 1918.

Army Form C. 2118.

D.A.D.V.S.
42ⁿᵈ Division.

WAR DIARY
INTELLIGENCE SUMMARY.
(Erase heading not required.)

Instructions regarding War Diaries and Intelligence Summaries are contained in F. S. Regs., Part II. and the Staff Manual respectively. Title pages will be prepared in manuscript.

Place	Date	Hour	Summary of Events and Information	Remarks and references to Appendices
LOCON	2-2-18		Attended Conference held by A.D.V.S. 1ˢᵗ Corps.	
BETHUNE CHARING	8-2-18		Attended Conference held by A.D.V.S. 1ˢᵗ Corps.	
SHEET 36ᵃSE, 36SW.	10-2-18		Capt. Concannon R.A.V.C. went to Hospital.	
36 NE. 36 NW.			Examined 90 Remounts for R.A.	
M1 cm X 7e 6 S	12-2-18		Examined 91 Remounts (70 Horses and 21 Mules)	
	13-2-18		Capt. O'Neill J.I. AVC arrived to replace Capt. Concannon.	
	15-2-18		Moved to HINGES	
HINGES	19-2-18		Examined 46 Remounts (Horses)	
W12 a 10.6.5	23-2-18		Attended Conference held by A.D.V.S. 1ˢᵗ Corps.	

JoGillies Major AVC
D.A.D.V.S. 42ⁿᵈ Divⁿ.

D.A.D.V.S. 42ⁿᵈ Division.

WAR DIARY.

Volume 3.

March 1ˢᵗ to March 31ˢᵗ 1918.

D.A.D.V.S.,
42nd DIVISION.
No. V/882
Date 1/4/18.

Army Form C. 2118.

D.A.D.V.S.
42nd DIVISION.

WAR DIARY
INTELLIGENCE SUMMARY.
(Erase heading not required.)

Instructions regarding War Diaries and Intelligence Summaries are contained in F. S. Regs., Part II. and the Staff Manual respectively. Title pages will be prepared in manuscript.

Place	Date	Hour	Summary of Events and Information	Remarks and references to Appendices
HINGES	1-3-18		126th Army Brigade R.F.A. situated at Mount Bernenchon W.1.a.5.5. came under my administration.	
BETHUNE Combined Sht 36A SE	2.3.18		Interview with D.V.S.	
36 SW 36A NE	4.3.18		Examined 176 Remounts (96 Horses and 80 Mules)	
36 C N.W.	5.3.18		Moved to La Beuvrière.	
MONT WIGNES				
LA BEUVRIÈRE	6.3.18		Visited 129th Coy. A.S.C. with A.D.V.S. 1st Corps re case of Epizootic Lymphangitis and gave instructions for A.F. W3738 to be carried out.	
Divd 2 in			Attended at 19th Mobile Veterinary Section when D.D.R. 1st Army held Casting Parade.	
	9.3.18		Attended Conference held by A.D.V.S. 1st Corps.	
	14-3-18		Examined 47 Remounts	
			Visited 19th M.V.S. and examined suspected case of Epizootic Lymphangitis – Rider from 437th Field Coy. R.E. Microscopic Examination – Negative.	
	16.3.18		Attended Conference held by A.D.V.S. 1st Corps.	
			Handed over to Major C.W. Godwin A.V.C.	
	17.3.18		Had interview with A.D.V.S. 1st Corps. Inspected Units P.L.	
	19.3.18		Inspected Surplus Remount Horses of 16 L.T.M.B.L.T. No. 1/92 with D.R.R. Cpls. P.L.	
	22.3.15		Acts as force in milk all following officers attached to France at Lillers held by D.V.S. 2nd E	
	23.3.18		Added to 1st BEF RA JEWISTIC WSA 352 P.L. and to STANDARD SHOEING PROCESS. P.L.	
C.AMIENS A.	26.3.18		12 Horses killed by Shell fire, 19 wounded, 3 of which had to be destroyed. P.L.	
KUSSEPH				
	31.3.18		5 Horses killed by Shell fire.	

G.H. Godwin Major A.V.C.
D.A.D.V.S. 42nd Division

D.A.D.V.S.
42ⁿᵈ DIVISION
WAR DIARY.
VOLUME 4

April 1ˢᵗ to April 30ᵗʰ 1918.

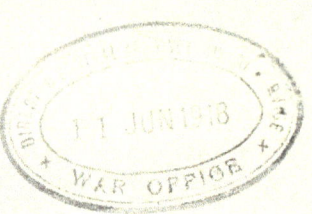

WAR DIARY or INTELLIGENCE SUMMARY

Army Form C. 2118.

D.A.D.V.S.
42nd Division

Instructions regarding War Diaries and Intelligence Summaries are contained in F.S. Regs., Part II. and the Staff Manual respectively. Title pages will be prepared in manuscript.

Place	Date	Hour	Summary of Events and Information	Remarks and references to Appendices
ST AMAND Sheet 57D SW.C.5.5	2/4/18		19h Mobile Veterinary Section moved from COUIN Sheet 57D to SOUASTRE Sheet 57D	R.F.
	3/4/18		Moved to HENU Sheet 57D C.24 b.6.9. happened to 20 animals, remounts for 42nd Division R.A. MC from Contagious disease.	R.F.
HENU	4/4/18		Sergeant SEDDON R.C.L. A.V.C. attached 126th Inf. Bde. admitted to hospital	R.F.
	5/4/18		Chief of R.A.D. HORSES, remounts for Division arrived to ADVS IV Corps at MARIEUX	R.F.
			Above consignment sent by ADVS IV Corps at MARIEUX	R.F.
	6/4/18		Moved from HENU to PAS Sheet 57D C.16.C.9.1. 19h Mobile Veterinary Section moved from SOUASTRE to PAS Sheet 57D C.16.a.3.3	R.F.
PAS	8/4/18		Sergeant HAYES, A.V.C. taken into duty from 2nd Veterinary Hospital and posted to 8th BDE. R.F.A. farrier. During night 10 HORSES were wounded by shell fire, 6 of these DIED, and 4 had to be destroyed. 15 MULES wounded by shell fire, 5 of	R.F.
			the above had to be destroyed.	R.F.
	11/4/18		Above animals were killed by ADVS IV Corps at MARIEUX	R.F.
	13/4/18		10th Mobile Veterinary Section moved to East End of Bois-de-ST PIERRE Sheet 57D C.22 b.5.0.	R.F.
	14/4/18		Moved to COUIN Sheet 57D T.10.6.8.	R.F.
	15/4/18		Remounts No 20 MULES. Remounts for M.G. Battalion T. Irish Coy R.E. Machine	R.F.
COUIN	16/4/18		Gun Guards, 22 HORSES were wounded by shell fire, 1/10 A.R. died (4 which had to be destroyed) 6 MULES were wounded by SHELL FIRE	R.F.
			33 HORSES were GASSED, 1 of which had to be destroyed	R.F.
	21/4/18		Horses & Mules taken by ADVS IV Corps at MARIEUX	R.F.
	25/4/18		All issued & loaned (one closed in accordance with D.D.V.S. THIRD ARMY AX 308. Wednesday 24/4/18 Surface animals on FOURTH ARMY DIED, suspected to result of eating Issued Cake. 63 HORSES evacuated by SHELL FIRE HOrses DIED, and IV DESTROYED. 8 HORSES GASSED, 1 of which had to be destroyed	R.F.
	2/5/18		1 MULE wounded by SHELL FIRE	R.F.
	3/4/18		1 MULE wounded by SHELL FIRE 1 MULE confirmed killed by NOVS IV Corps at MARIEUX	R.F.
			Supplied Milk Requisite to Division ALL Returns from Contagious Diseases	R.F.
			Cyst Sergeant R.W. OWEN A.V.C. reported on duty from No 2 Veterinary Hospital and posted to 126th Inf. Bde.	R.F.

G.W. Jordan, Major A.V.C.
D.A.D.V.S. 42nd Division

D.A.D.V.S.
42nd Division.
War Diary.

Volume 5

May 1st 1918 to May 31st 1918

D.A.D.V.S.,
42nd DIVISION.

War Diary
D.A.D.V.S.
42nd Division.

VOLUME 6.

June 1st 1918 to June 30th 1918.

D.A.D.V.S.,
42nd DIVISION.
No. V2130
Date 1-7-18

Army Form C. 2118.

WAR DIARY
or
INTELLIGENCE SUMMARY.

(Erase heading not required.)

Instructions regarding War Diaries and Intelligence Summaries are contained in F. S. Regs., Part II. and the Staff Manual respectively. Title pages will be prepared in manuscript.

Place	Date	Hour	Summary of Events and Information	Remarks and references to Appendices
PAS	1-6-18		Attended conference held by ADVS IV Corps at MARIEUX. Q.g	
Sheet 57dD C.6.a.2.3	5-6-18		Inspected G.D. and H.D. Horses. Remounts for the 30th American Ins. Regs. All free from Contagious disease. Q.g	
	6-6-18		For the week ending the 6-6-18. 1 Horse was killed by Shell fire, and 4 wounded, 1 of which had to be destroyed. Q.g	
BUS-LE-ARTOIS Sheet 57d			Moved to BUS-LE-ARTOIS Sheet 57d J 26 a 9.3 196 Mobile Veterinary Section moved to LOUVENCOURT Sheet 57d T 33 a 1.8. Q.g	
57d.J.26.a.9.3	12-6-18		Attended conference held by ADVS IV Corps at MARIEUX Q.g	
	13-6-18		Inspected 1 Brigade remount for G.S.O I 42nd Division Q.g	
	15-6-18		For the week ending 13-6-18, 2 horses were wounded by Shell fire, 1 wounded by Gunshot, and 2 slightly gassed by Mustard Gas Q.g	
	19-6-18		Attended conference held by ADVS IV Corps at MARIEUX. Q.g	
	21-6-18		Inspected H/D horses and Mules, remounts for Division. All free from Contagious Disease Q.g	
	22-6-18		Attended conference held by ADVS IV Corps at MARIEUX. Q.g	
	27-6-18		Isolated 3 Officers chargers, remounts. All free from Contagious Disease. Q.g	
	30-6-18		Inspected 10 Riding Horses, 10 Mules, and 10 H/D Mules, remounts for Division. All free from Contagious Disease Q.g	

D.S.O.
30.6.18

C.W.Godwin Major AVC
DADVS
42nd Division.

War Diary.

Volume 7.

From 1-7-18.
To 31-7-18.

D.A.D.V.S. 42ND DIVISION.

D.A.D.V.S.,
42nd DIVISION.
No. V 2194
Date 1-8-18.

WAR DIARY
~~INTELLIGENCE~~ SUMMARY
(Erase heading not required.)

Army Form C. 2118.

Instructions regarding War Diaries and Intelligence Summaries are contained in F. S. Regs., Part II. and the Staff Manual respectively. Title pages will be prepared in manuscript.

Place	Date	Hour	Summary of Events and Information	Remarks and references to Appendices
BUS-LES-ARTOIS	3.4.18		Major Godwin E.W. D.A.D.V.S. 42nd Division proceeded on 14 days leave	
	4.4.18		6 Officers Chargers, Remounts for the Division. Inspected and found free from Contagious Disease. For week ending the 4.4.18. 1 Horse was wounded by Shell fire, and 1 Gassed.	App
	6.4.18		4 Officers Chargers, Remounts for the Division. Inspected and found one from Contagious Disease	App
	9.4.18		14 R.D. Horses, 1 V.D. Mules, 11 H.D. Horses, 11.H.D. Mules, Remounts for the Division. Inspected also found free from Contagious Disease.	App
	9.4.18		Horse & Scabies was Returned Sheet 57D Scale 40000 4.11 a 5.4.	App
SARTON	11.4.18		For the week ending 11.4.18, 1 Horse wounded by Shell fire, and one wounded by Gunshot.	App
			1 Mule wounded by Gunshot.	App
	16.4.18		Moved to AUTHIE Mobveterinr Sheet 57D Scale 40000 C.16.a.5.2.	App
	18.4.18		Major Godwin E.W. D.A.D.V.S. 42nd Division returned from 14 days leave. For the week ending the 18.4.18, 1 Horse was killed by Shell fire, and 1 Mule wounded by Shell fire.	App
	20.4.18		Attended conference held by A.D.V.S. IV Corps at MARIEUX	App
	25.4.18		For the week ending the 25.4.18, 1 Horse wounded by Gunshot, and 1 Mule killed by Shell fire.	App
	27.4.18		Attended conference held by A.D.V.S. VII Corps at MARIEUX	App

G.H. Godwin
30.4.18

G.H. Godwin
Major A.V.C.
D.A.D.V.S.
42nd Division

WAR DIARY.

VOLUME 8

August 1st to August 31st 1918.

D.A.D.V.S. 42nd Division.

> D.A.D.V.S., 42nd DIVISION.
> No. V2291
> Date 2-9-18.

Army Form C. 2118.

WAR DIARY
or
INTELLIGENCE SUMMARY
(Erase heading not required.)

Instructions regarding War Diaries and Intelligence Summaries are contained in F. S. Regs., Part II. and the Staff Manual respectively. Title pages will be prepared in manuscript.

Place	Date	Hour	Summary of Events and Information	Remarks and references to Appendices
AUTHIE Sheet 57^D 1/1 6a 32	1-9-18		For the week ending 1-9-18, 1 Horse was Killed by Shell fire. G.W.G.	
	3-9-18		The following Remounts arrived for the Division, and were found fit for duty (Contagious Diseases) 31 Redens, 13 L.D.H., 13 L.D.M. Captain Road proceeded on 14 days leave. G.W.G.	
	8-9-18		For the week ending 8-9-18, 1 Mule was wounded by Shellfire, and 3 Horses wounded by Shell fire. G.W.G.	
	10-9-18		Attended horses killed by A.D.V.S. 7th Corps at MARIEUX. The following remounts arrived for the Division, and were found fit from Contagious Diseases 4 Redens, 4 LDH, 6 LDM, 5 YD. Total 22. G.W.G.	
	15-9-18		For the week ending 15-9-18, 1 Mule again wounded by Shell fire. Moves to BUS-LE-ARTOIS Sheet 57^D 4000 J.26.a.8.2. G.W.G.	
BUS	22-9-18		Attended Conference held by A.D.V.S. 7th Corps at MARIEUX. Cabriolard A.V.C. arrived back from 14 days leave. G.W.G.	
	22-9-18		For the week ending 22-9-18, 5 Horses and 1 Mule were wounded by Shell fire. 2 Horses killed by Shell fire. Captain Jones A.V.C. O.C. 19th Mobile Veterinary Section proceeded on 14 days leave to U.K. G.W.G.	
	24-9-18		The following Remounts arrived for the Division, and were found free from Contagious Diseases. 2 Redens and 30 L.D. Horses. G.W.G.	
	26-9-18		19th Mobile Vety. Section moved to BERTRANCOURT. Sheet 57^D 4000 P. G.W.G.	
	27-9-18		19th Mobile Vety. Section moved to Sugar factory. Sheet 57^D 4000 K 33 a 6.5. G.W.G.	
	29-9-18		For the week ending 29-9-18 5 Horses and 1 Mule were killed (one to exploration of mine), and 6 Horses wounded. 13 Horses and 4 Mules were killed by Shellfire. 10 Horses and 6 Mules G.W.G.	
	30-9-18 31-9-18		wounded by Shell fire. 19th Mobile Vety. Section moved to MIRAUMONT Sheet 57^D L 35 c 5.3 G.W.G. Moved to MIRAUMONT Sheet 57^D L 35 c 5.3 G.W.G.	

G.W.G.
Major A.V.C.
D.A.D.V.S.

G.W. Godwin

WAR DIARY
VOLUME 9.

From 1.9.18 to 30.9.18

D.A.D.V.S. 42nd DIVISION.

D.A.D.V.S., 42nd DIVISION.
No. V2305
Date 30-9-18

Army Form C. 2118.

WAR DIARY
or
INTELLIGENCE SUMMARY.
(Erase heading not required.)

Instructions regarding War Diaries and Intelligence Summaries are contained in F. S. Regs., Part II. and the Staff Manual respectively. Title pages will be prepared in manuscript.

Place	Date	Hour	Summary of Events and Information	Remarks and references to Appendices
MIRAUMONT Sh 57 D L.35.C.5.3 PYS.			Moved to PYS. Sh 57 C. 20.00 M.2.C.5.5. EU.Y	
	5.9.18		To commencing 5.9.18 47 horses were killed and 41 wounded by shellfire. 11 mules killed, and 16 wounded by shellfire. EU.Y	
	6.9.18		The following Remounts arrived for the Division, and were found to be free from Contagious Disease. 32 LD Horses, 28 LD Mules, and 2ND horses. Remounts examined held by ADVS IV Corps at GREVILLERS EU.Y	
	7.9.18			
	8.9.18		To the ensuring M.O.R. Horse was killed and 5 wounded by shellfire. 1 Mule killed and 2 wounded by shellfire. EU.Y	
	9.9.18		Captain O'Neill of report sick for 14 days, Gone to UK. EU.Y	
	10.9.18		To the week ending 14.9.18. 63 horses were killed by bombs, 5 killed by shellfire, 49 wounded by bombs, and 4 wounded by shellfire. 13 Mules killed by bombs, and 16 wounded by bombs. EU.Y	
	15.9.18		40 Mules Remounts to Division will arrive free from Contagious Disease EU.Y	
	21.9.18		Moved to Continuer held by ADVS IV Corps at GREVILLERS. Moved 8 LEBUCQUIERE Map reference I.24.d.1.3. Sh 57c c /40000. EU.Y	
LEBUCQUIERE 21.9.18			To the Following Remounts arrived -01 to Division, and were examined found Contagious Disease.	
	27.9.18		For the week ending 21.9.18. 11 Horses were killed, and 28 wounded by shellfire. 4 mules killed and 4 wounded by shellfire. EU.Y	
	28.9.18		The following Remounts arrived for the Division, and were held free from Contagious Disease. 32 LD Horses & 2 LD Mules. EU.Y	

G.N. Godwin Major H.C.
A.D.V.S. 42nd Division

30.9.18.

WAR DIARY

VOLUME 10

16/21

D.A.D.V.S.,
42nd DIVISION.
No. V2076
Date 1/11/18

From 1/10/18 to 31/10/18

D.A.D.V.S. 42nd Division

Army Form C. 2118.

WAR DIARY
or
INTELLIGENCE=SUMMARY.
(Erase heading not required.)

Instructions regarding War Diaries and Intelligence Summaries are contained in F. S. Regs., Part II. and the Staff Manual respectively. Title pages will be prepared in manuscript.

Place	Date	Hour	Summary of Events and Information	Remarks and references to Appendices
LEBUCQUIERE	1/10/18		Inspection of Wagon Lines of Nos.1,2 & S.A.A.Section D.A.C. Office moved to I36.d.8.1. Sheet 57c 1/40000.	JWC
I 36.d.8.1.	2/10/18		Inspection of Wagon Lines of 126th.&127th.Infantry Bdes.,1/7th.Northumberland Fusiliers (P),& 428th.Field Coy.R.E.	JWC
--do--	3/10/18		Inspection of Wagon Lines of 210th.&211th.Brigades R.F.A.	JWC
--do--	4/10/18		Conference with V.Os. Inspection of Wagon Lines of Nos 2,3.&4 Coys.A.S.C.	JWC
--do--	5/10/18		Conference at IVth.Corps. Inspection of Remounts.	JWC
--do--	6/10/18		Meeting Remounts at YTRES Railhead, and inspection of same.	JWC
--do--	7/10/18		Accompanying A.D.V.S.IVth.Corps on inspection of 317th.Bde.R.F.A.& Remounts in 210th.Bde.R.F.A., and Nos.1&2 Sections D.A.C.	JWC
--do--	8/10/18		Meeting Remounts at FREMICOURT Railhead and inspecting same, & ordinary Routine.	JWC
--do--	9/10/18		Moved from I 36.d.8.1. to TRESCAULT and on to ESNES. Move of 19th.M.V.S. from RUYAULCOURT to TRESCAULT.	JWC
ESNES.	10/10/18		Routine duty. Move of 19th.M.V.S. from TRESCAULT to Pont et Esc° M.5.c.8.8. Sheet 57b 1/40000.	JWC
--do--	11/10/18		Conference with V.Os. and Routine duty.	JWC
--do--	12/10/18		Move from ESNES to BEAUVOIS. Move of 19th.M.V.S. from Pont et Ec°se. to H.33.b.5.5. Sheet 57b 1/40000.	JWC
BEAUVOIS	13/10/18		Routine and inspecting Wagon Lines of 428th.&429th.Field Coys.R.E. and 1/2nd.Field Ambulance.	JWC
--do--	14/10/18		Move of 19th.M.V.S. from H.33.b.5.5. to BEAUVOIS I.4.c.4.4.	JWC
--do--	15/10/18		Inspection of Wagon Lines of 1/1st.Field Ambulance and A&B Coys. M.G.C.	JWC
--do--	16/10/18		Routine and inspecting 23 Remounts(Riders) arriving at MARCOING. Inspection Wagon Lines of Nos. 1, 2, & S.A.A.Sections D.A.C.	JWC
--do--	17/10/18		Visit RUYAULCOURT and Inspecting Wagon Lines of 1/3rd.Fld.Ambulance.	JWC
--do--	18/10/18		Conference with V.Os. Inspecting Wagon Lines of 1/5th.&1/7th.Manchesters.	JWC
--do--	19/10/18		Visit RUMILLY Railhead to meet Remounts.	JWC
--do--	20&21/10/18		Routine and Inspecting Wagon Lines of 210th.Bde.R.F.A.	JWC
--do--	22&23/10/18		Routine and Inspecting Transport Lines of 1/5th.&1/7th.Lancashire Fusiliers.	JWC
--do--	24/10/18		Inspection of Transport Lines of 42nd.Bn.M.G.C.and 125th Inf.Bde.	JWC
--do--	25/10/18		Conference with V.Os.and inspecting Transport Lines of 429th.Coy.R.E.	JWC
--do--	26/10/18		Conference at A.D.V.S. IVth.Corps. Inspecting Transport Lines of 427th.and428th.Fld.Coys.R.E.	JWC
--do--	27/10/18		Inspecting Wagon Lines of A Battery 210th.Bde.R.F.A.	JWC
--do--	28&29/10/18		Inspecting Wagon Lines of B.C.& D.Batteries 210th.Bde.R.F.A. and 211th.Bde.R.F.A.	JWC
--do--	30/10/18		Inspecting Transport Lines of 1/1st.1/2nd.&1/3rd.Field Ambulances.	JWC
--do--	31/10/18		Inspecting Transport Lines of 126th.& 127th.Inf.Bdes.	JWC

JW Connell
Major A.V.C.,
D.A.D.V.S., 42nd.DIVISION

War Diary.
Volume II.

Shows 1/11/18 to 30/7/18

D.A.D.V.S.
42nd Division

D.A.D.V.S.
42nd DIVISION.
No. V2589
Date 1/2/18

Army Form C. 2118.

WAR DIARY
or
INTELLIGENCE-SUMMARY.
(Erase heading not required.)

Instructions regarding War Diaries and Intelligence Summaries are contained in F. S. Regs., Part II. and the Staff Manual respectively. Title pages will be prepared in manuscript.

Place	Date	Hour	Summary of Events and Information	Remarks and references to Appendices
BEAUVOIS	1/11/18		Conference of Veterinary Officers with	J.C.
"	2/11/18		Inspected Remounts	J.C.
"	3/11/18 to 4/11/18		Routine and Inspecting 143 Remounts. 19th M.V.S. moved from BEAUVOIS to SOLESMES.	J.C.
"	5/11/18		Moved from BEAUVOIS to POTELLE and on to LE QUESNOY.	J.C.
LE QUESNOY	6/11/18		Move of 19th. Mobile Veterinary Section from BEAUVOIS to LE QUESNOY. SOLESMES	J.C.
"	7/11/18		Routine	J.C.
"	8/11/18		Conference with Veterinary Officers. Visit to advanced Headquarters at HAUTE RUE to select site for 19th.Mobile Veterinary Section.	J.C.
"	9/11/18		Conference at A.D.V.S. IVth.Corps. Move of 19th.Mobile Veterinary Section from LE QUESNOY to HARGNIES.	J.C.
"	10/11/18		Moved from LE QUESNOY to HAUTMONT.	J.C.
HAUTMONT	11/11/18		Conference at 42nd.D.H.Q. Inspected stables in neighbourhood of HAUTMONT. Armistice declared at 1100 hours.	J.C.
"	12&13/11/18		Routine and Inspecting Transport Lines of 427th.428th.and 429th.Fld.Coy.R.E.	J.C.
"	14/11/18		Inspecting Transport Lines of 42nd.Divisional Signal Coy.and Divisional Headquarters	J.C.
"	15/11/18		Conference with Veterinary Officers. Inspecting Transport Lines of 42nd.Bn.M.G.C.	J.C.
"	16&17/11/18		Inspecting Wagon Lines of 210th.Bde.R.F.A.	J.C.
"	18/11/18		Inspecting Wagon Lines of 211th.Bde.R.F.A., and 20 Remounts.	J.C.
"	19/11/18		Inspecting Transport Lines of 125th. and 126th.Infantry Bdes.	J.C.
"	20/11/18		Inspecting Transport Lines of 127th.Infantry Bde.	J.C.
"	21/11/18		Inspecting Wagon Lines of D.A.C.	J.C.
"	22/11/18		Conference with Veterinary Officers. Inspecting Transport Lines of I/1st.I/2nd.&I/3rd.Fld.Ambs.	J.C.
"	23/11/18		Inspecting Transport Lines of I/7th.North'd Fus.(P) & No I Coy.A.S.C.	J.C.
"	24&25/11/18		Inspecting Wagon Lines of No 3 Coy.A.S.C. Inspecting 63 Remounts.	J.C.
"	26/11/18		Inspecting Wagon Lines of A.& D Batteries 210th.Bde.R.F.A.& 211th.Bde.R.F.A.	J.C.
"	27/11/18		Inspecting Transport Lines of Nos.2&4 Coys.A.S.C.	J.C.
"	28/11/18		Conference with Veterinary Officers. Selecting Mares with Committee to be earmarked for breeding purposes	J.C.
"	29/11/18		Inspecting Mares for breeding purposes with Committee.	J.C.
"	30/11/18		Inspecting Mares for breeding purposes with Committee.	J.C.

J.C.Connell.

Major A.V.C.,
D.A.D.V.S.
42nd.DIVISION

WAR DIARY.
VOLUME 12.
D.A.D.V.S. 42ND DIVISION.

From 1/12/18 to 31/12/18.

D.A.D.V.S.
42nd DIVISION.
No. 1/26.25
Date 1/1/19

Army Form C. 2118.

WAR DIARY
or
INTELLIGENCE SUMMARY.
(Erase heading not required.)

Instructions regarding War Diaries and Intelligence Summaries are contained in F. S. Regs., Part II. and the Staff Manual respectively. Title pages will be prepared in manuscript.

Place	Date	Hour	Summary of Events and Information	Remarks and references to Appendices
HAUTMONT	1/12/18		Visit of Sir Harry to KING	
	2/12/18		Inspecting Horses with Committee for breeding purposes, and inspected remounts	
	3/12/18		Inspecting Horses with Committee for breeding purposes	
	4/12/18		Inspecting 10% Mobile Veterinary Station, and interview breeding purposes with Committee	
	5/12/18		Inspecting transport lines of H.A.B. 4.B.B. & H.Q.O.S. Field Coys. R.E.	
	6/12/18		Inspecting Wagon Lines of 2nd & 152 nd Batteries 84 & Bde. R.G.A.	
	7 & 8/12/18		Inspecting Wagon Lines of No 1 Coy A.S.C. and H/4 Yorks Bde. (?)	
	9/12/18		Inspecting Wagon Lines of H/106 Bde. R.F.A. and D/245 Bde. R.F.A.	
	10/12/18		Inspecting Wagon Lines of A, B & C Batteries 211 & Bde. R.F.A.	
	11/12/18		Inspecting Wagon Lines of A.B. C. Batteries 311 & 12 nd Bde. R.F.A.	
	12/12/18		Inspecting transport Lines of 125 & 128 nd Coys. A.S.C.	
	13/12/18		Conference with No 1 Tésin to CHARLEROI & THEURES & inspect stations	
	14/12/18		en route	
	15/12/18		Inspecting 310 & 248 Bde. R.F.A. D.A.C. & A & D R.H. Ammn. Sec. R. H.Q. with B.O.C on line of march. Move of	
BINCHE	16/12/18		10% Mobile Vety Section from HAUTMONT & BINCHE. 10% Mobile Vety Section moved from HARPENT & LOBBES	
FONTAINE L'EVEQUE	17/12/18		Visit Div. moved from HAUTMONT & BINCHE	
	18/12/18		His Grace moved from BINCHE & FONTAINE L'EVEQUE	
	19/12/18		Review.	
	20/12/18		Div. O.Pro moved from FONTAINE L'EVEQUE to CHARLEROI. 10 %. A.C. moved from LOBBES & GILLY	
CHARLEROI	21/12/18		Conference with A.O.S	
	22/12/18		Inspecting Wagon Lines of H.Q. 2 nd Bn. Marine Gun Corps.	
	23/12/18		Inspecting Wagon Lines of D/106 & 248 Bdes R.F.A.	
	24/12/18		Inspecting Wagon Lines of Nos 2, 3 & 4 Coys. A.S.C.	
	25/12/18		Inspecting Wagon Lines of Field Amb. Cases.	
	26/12/18		Xmas Day. Routine and inspecting mount numbers at 10% R.E.	
	27/12/18		Conference with A.O.S	
	28/12/18		Inspecting animals of 2 nd Army Bde. R. F. A.	
	29/12/18		Conduct inspection of Wagon Lines 86 & 42 nd Bty. Boyd Horse Coy R.E.	
	30/12/18		Inspecting Transport units of 8 nd Bde. Horse	
	31/12/18		Inspecting Wagon Lines of D.A.C	

C. Farrell
Major R.A.V.C
R.A. Division

WAR DIARY

D.A.D.V.S.

42nd Division

VOLUME 1.

Jan 1st 1919 Jan. 31st 1919

Army Form C. 2118.

WAR DIARY
or
INTELLIGENCE SUMMARY.
(Erase heading not required.)

Instructions regarding War Diaries and Intelligence Summaries are contained in F. S. Regs., Part II. and the Staff Manual respectively. Title pages will be prepared in manuscript.

Place	Date	Hour	Summary of Events and Information	Remarks and references to Appendices
CHARLEROI	1-1-19		Roads in J.C.	
	2-1-19		Covered with Veterinary Officers J.C.	
	3-4-19 & 8-9/19		Classifying animals	
	5/1/19		Conference with Veterinary Officer in reference to R.V.S.C.	
	10-1-19 & 13/1/19		Conference with Veterinary Officer and carrying animals R.V.S.C.	
	14/1/19		Classifying animals	
	15/1/19		Conference with Veterinary Officer and carrying animals R.V.S.C.	
	17/1/19 to 22/1/19		Classifying animals	
	23/1/19		Conference with Veterinary Officer and carrying animals	
	24/1/19 to 25/1/19		Classifying animals	
	27/1/19		Conference with Veterinary Officer	
	28/1/19		Visit carrying out Veterinary arrangements and animals of 16th Lancers Regiment & conferring with Veterinary Officers	
	30/1/19		Inspection with Veterinary Officer Inspecting animals of 21st R.C. J.C. L.A. J.C.	
	31/1/19		Conference in reference to sick Racehorses R.V.S.	

J Schmitt
Major R.A.V.C.
A.D.V.S.
4 Division

WAR DIARY.

D.A.D.V.S. 42nd Division

VOLUME 2.

from 1/2/19 to 28/2/19

Army Form C. 2118.

WAR DIARY
or
INTELLIGENCE SUMMARY.
(Erase heading not required.)

Instructions regarding War Diaries and Intelligence Summaries are contained in F. S. Regs., Part II. and the Staff Manual respectively. Title pages will be prepared in manuscript.

Place	Date	Hour	Summary of Events and Information	Remarks and references to Appendices
Charlerol	1/2/19 to 4/2/19		Routine.	
"	5/2/19		14 Brood Mares (Including 3 Superlative) left Division for Dieppe.	
"	6/2/19		Conference with Veterinary Officers and Routine.	
"	7/2/19 to 9/2/19		Routine	
"	10/2/19		Inspected animals sent to IVth. Veterinary Evacuation Station for sale, chiefly Blind, Specific Ophthalmia, and D- Cases	
"	11/2/19		Inspected 120 animals marked "Y" for repatriation to England	
"	12/2/19		Inspected 120 animals marked "Y" for repatriation to England at Railhead Charlerol.	
"	13/2/19		Conference with Veterinary Officers and classifying 4 animals at Montigny	
"	14/2/19		Attended conference at A.D.V.S.Office IVth.Corps Warre.	
"	15/2/19		Inspected 104 animals marked "Y" for repatriation to England	
"	16/2/19		Inspected "Y" animals of R.Es for repatriation to England	
"	17/2/19		Routine	
"	18/2/19		Routine	
"	19/2/19		Attended sale of 100 animals marked "Z" at Charlerol.	
"	20/2/19		Inspected 108 animals marked "Z" at 19th.Mobile Veterinary Section for sale on 21/2/19. Received payment for animals sold on 19/2/19 and handed same over to Field Cashier IVth Corps. Conference with Veterinary Officers.	
"	21/2/19		Attended sale of 107 animals marked "Z" at Charlerol. Inspected 88 animals marked "Y" for repatriation to England at Railhead Charlerol.	
"	22&23/2/19		Routine	
"	24/2/19		Inspected "Y" animals for repatriation to England at Railhead Charlerol.	
"	25/2/19		Attended sale of 124 animals marked "Z" at Charlerol.	
"	26/2/19		Routine	
"	27/2/19		Conference with Veterinary Officers and attended sale of 60 animals marked "Z" at Gilly.	
"	28/2/19		Routine.	

J C Burrell

Major R.A.V.C.,
D.A.D.V.S.,
42nd.Division

War Diary.
Volume 3.
D.A.D.V.S. 42nd Divn

1/3/19 to 31/3/19

Army Form C. 2118.

WAR DIARY
or
INTELLIGENCE=SUMMARY.
(Erase heading not required.)

Instructions regarding War Diaries and Intelligence Summaries are contained in F. S. Regs., Part II. and the Staff Manual respectively. Title pages will be prepared in manuscript.

Place	Date MARCH	Hour	Summary of Events and Information	Remarks and references to Appendices
CHARLEROI	1		Attended sale of 75 Z Animals at CHARLEROI	
"	2		Routine	
"	3		Inspecting 150 Z animals proceeding to the 4th.Veterinary Evacuating Station GEMBLOUX	
"	4		Attended sale of 95 Z Animals at CHARLEROI	
"	5		Inspecting 150 Z animals proceeding to the 4th.Veterinary Evacuating Station GEMBLOUX	
"	6		Conference with Veterinary Officers, and inspecting 61 Y animals proceeding to Base	
"	7		Attended sale of 49 Z Animals at CHARLEROI	
"	8		Attended sale of 120 Z Animals at CHARLEROI	
"	9		Inspecting 150 Z animals proceeding to 4th.Veterinary Evacuating Station GEMBLOUX	
"	10		Captain LORD H.H. R.A.V.C. proceeded on 14 days leave to United Kingdom	
"	11		Attended sale of 68 Z animals at CHARLEROI. Inspected 152 Z animals proceeding to Base.	
"	12		Inspected 150 Z animals proceeding to the 4th.Veterinary Evacuating Station GEMBLOUX.	
"	13		Inspected 150 Z animals proceeding to the 4th.Veterinary Evacuating Station GEMBLOUX.	
"	14to19		Attended sale of 62 Z animals at CHARLEROI, and Conference with Veterinary Officers.	
"	20		Routine	
"	21		Conference with Veterinary Officers.	
"	22		One Sergeant and eight Privates R.A.V.C. proceeded to the 4th.Veterinary Evacuating Station GEMBLOUX for duty.	
"	23		Routine	
"	24		Inspected 243 X animals proceeding to HAVRE	
"	25		Inspected 96 X animals proceeding to HAVRE	
"	26		Captain LORD H.H. R.A.V.C. returned from 14 days leave in U.K.	
"	27		Major CONNELL J.A. R.A.V.C. proceeded for Demobilization	
"	28		Conference with Veterinary Officers	
"	29		Inspected 217 X Animals proceeding to R.G.A.Units	
"	30		Captain FRAYNE G. R.A.V.C. proceeded for duty to 8th.Division Second Army.	
"	31		Routine	
"			Inspected 225 Animals proceeding to OUTREAU, also 96 Animals proceeding to NIVELLES.	

H.H. Lord Captain R.A.V.C.,
A/D.A.D.V.S.,
42nd.DIVISION.

www.ingramcontent.com/pod-product-compliance
Lightning Source LLC
Chambersburg PA
CBHW081244170426
43191CB00034B/2036